Essential Viewpoints

Performance-Enhancing Drugs

Essential Viewpoints

PERFORMANCE-ENHANCING
DRUGS
BY TOM ROBINSON

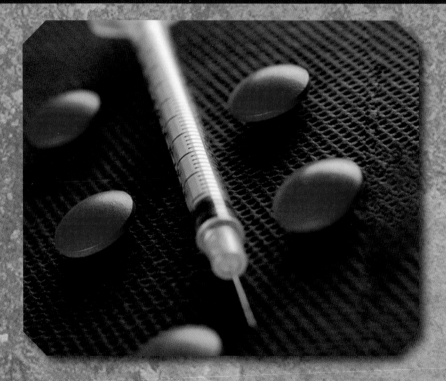

Content Consultant
Mikhail G. Epshteyn, Doctor of Pharmacy
Director of Pharmacy Services,
Regency Hospital of Minneapolis

ABDO
Publishing Company

CREDITS

Published by ABDO Publishing Company, 8000 West 78th Street, Edina, Minnesota 55439. Copyright © 2009 by Abdo Consulting Group, Inc. International copyrights reserved in all countries. No part of this book may be reproduced in any form without written permission from the publisher. The Essential Library™ is a trademark and logo of ABDO Publishing Company.

Printed in the United States.

Editor: Amy Van Zee
Copy Editor: Paula Lewis
Interior Design and Production: Ryan Haugen
Cover Design: Becky Daum

Library of Congress Cataloging-in-Publication Data
Robinson, Tom.
  Performance-enhancing drugs / by Tom Robinson.
     p. cm. — (Essential viewpoints)
  Includes bibliographical references and index.
  ISBN 978-1-60453-111-4
  1. Doping in sports—Juvenile literature. 2. Anabolic steroids—Juvenile literature. I. Title.

  RC1230.R62 2009
  362.29—dc22

                              2008007012

TABLE OF CONTENTS

San Francisco Giants outfielder Barry Bonds hit his 756th career home run on August 7, 2007.

TAINTED HISTORY

arry Bonds stood at home plate admiring the result of his incredible strength. Bonds watched the baseball soar over the fence and into history at the deepest point of the San Francisco Giants' ballpark.

He raised his arms triumphantly and headed off to circle the bases while family members began making their way to home plate to be part of the celebration.

Salutes and congratulations followed the 756th home run in Bonds's Major League Baseball career. However, there was also controversy swirling around the San Francisco Giants slugger before and after he completed his pursuit of Hank Aaron's career home run record. The record had stood as one of the most prestigious in sports for 33 years.

Bonds became baseball's Home Run King in the fifth inning of the Giants' 8–6 loss to the Washington Nationals on August 7, 2007. "I knew I hit it," Bonds said. "I knew I got it. I was like, phew, finally."[1] The home run, however, did not represent the end of the road. After the ball left his bat after a one-out,

The Nature of Competition

Observers of Barry Bonds trace his use of performance-enhancing drugs to his anger over the attention Mark McGwire received for crushing the single-season home run record by hitting 70 in 1998.

While playing for the St. Louis Cardinals, McGwire easily broke the home run record of 61 set by Roger Maris of the New York Yankees in 1961. McGwire was briefly involved in controversy during his home run pursuit when a reporter noticed androstenedione (also known as "andro"), an over-the-counter dietary supplement, in his locker. Andro, a hormone that is a precursor to testosterone, acts like a steroid and was already banned in some other sports. Although legal at the time, andro is currently banned by the U.S. Food and Drug Administration for its significant health risks.

full-count pitch from Mike Bacsik, the result continued to fuel one of the most volatile debates in the history of sports.

THE HEART OF THE CONTROVERSY

Suspicions that Bonds may have used steroids and other performance-enhancing drugs to aid his chase for the home-run record were at the center of the heated debate. "This record is not tainted at all," Bonds said the night of his record-breaking home run. "At all. Period."[3]

Others disagreed. Although baseball commissioner Bud Selig offered a congratulatory statement, Selig was noticeably absent on the record-breaking night. Even Selig's message acknowledged the controversy that followed Bonds and his status as the subject of an investigation into whether he had lied to a grand jury about whether he ever used steroids.

In his statement, Selig said:

I congratulate Barry Bonds for establishing a new, career home run record. Barry's achievement is noteworthy and remarkable. While the issues which have swirled around this record will continue to work themselves toward resolution, today is a day for congratulations on a truly remarkable achievement.[4]

Bonds may have been relieved that the chase to break the record was over, but the debate was only beginning. His name had come up repeatedly in reports about his 2003 testimony given during a grand jury investigation. The investigation looked into the distribution of steroids and

In the Shadows

Mark Fainaru-Wada and Lance Williams provided much of the reporting that tied Barry Bonds to investigations of performance-enhancing drugs. The two reporters wrote *Game of Shadows*, which documents the alleged details.

Sports Illustrated published excerpts from the book. The magazine wrote:

Beginning in 1998 with injections in his buttocks of Winstrol, a powerful steroid, Barry Bonds took a wide array of performance-enhancing drugs over at least five seasons in a massive doping regimen that grew more sophisticated as the years went on, according to Game of Shadows, *a book written by two San Francisco Chronicle reporters. . . .*

The authors . . . describe in sometimes day-to-day, drug-by-drug detail how often and how deeply Bonds engaged in the persistent doping. For instance, the authors write that by 2001, when Bonds broke Mark McGwire's single-season home-run record (70) by belting 73, Bonds was using two designer steroids referred to as the Cream and the Clear, as well as insulin, human growth hormone, testosterone decanoate . . . and trenbolone, a steroid created to improve the muscle quality of cattle.[5]

other illegal drugs by the Bay Area Laboratory Co-Operative (BALCO) and its founder Victor Conte. Federal agents raided BALCO's Burlingame, California, offices September 3, 2003, and uncovered documents that allegedly detailed Bonds's regimen of performance-enhancing drug use.

While Bonds continued to deny that he had ever knowingly used performance-enhancing drugs, the debate raged on. Was it possible that the noticeable changes in his physical build were the result of workouts or were the changes proof of chemical enhancement? As he got older, instead of slowing down like most baseball players, Barry Bonds began hitting homers at almost double the rate of his younger years.

Not Alone

The questions extend beyond Bonds to the general concern that the recent trend of soaring home run totals was the result of drugs rather

Victor Conte, founder of BALCO, holds a picture of Barry Bonds.

than exceptional athletes. More of baseball's big names, including Roger Clemens and teammate Andy Pettitte, surfaced in an internal investigation. Clemens had also posted almost unbelievable statistics well into his forties. The sport was once again under government scrutiny.

The Mitchell Report, compiled for baseball by former Senator George Mitchell, was released on December 13, 2007. The report attempted to analyze the depth of steroid problems in baseball.

COMPLICATED ISSUE

The apparent abundance of drugs in sports raises many questions.

The use of performance-enhancing drugs can be viewed as a question of ethics. If the drugs are used in a way to circumvent the rules of the sport, there is cheating involved. In most cases, the drugs used to enhance athletic performance are illegal except when prescribed for specific medical situations.

Beyond legal matters are issues of public health. Reports indicate that dangerous side effects cause long-term health concerns for users. There are also questions of whether famous athletes using the drugs will lead to more young athletes following in their footsteps.

A common perception is that athletes who have used drugs to improve their performance are combining their natural talent with unnatural, illegal, and dangerous chemicals. Still others think that what athletes do with their bodies is their own business. The issues surrounding performance-enhancing drug use include legal, health, and privacy matters, making it a complex question.

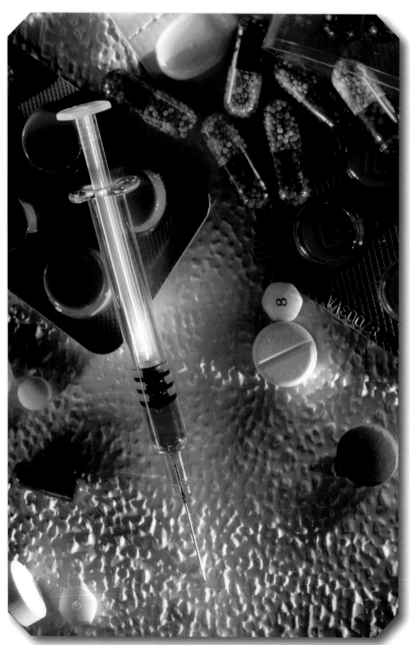

Performance-enhancing drugs come in numerous forms. Many are injected into the body, while some are ingested in pill form.

Ripped Fuel, a supplement containing ephedra, has been banned by the National Football League.

THE TEMPTATION

thletes put in hours, days, and weeks of training, all with the hope that improved performance will be the ultimate reward. The nature of competition and the thrill of winning often provide the needed motivation. Add the potential for fame and fortune, and athletes have more incentive to push themselves to greater heights.

In addition to the time spent working out and practicing, there are other ways to get ahead. Clearly, proper nutrition and good health can give an athlete better tools in the form of a stronger body. Theories abound about possible help from vitamins and nutritional supplements. Performance-enhancing drugs are viewed by some as the next step in that progression, a way to keep fine-tuning the body in pursuit of athletic accomplishment.

Complicating the decision process at times is the thought that the athletes one competes against may already be pursuing performance-enhancing drug options. By not pursuing such options, an athlete may be giving up a competitive edge to someone who is.

The Cost of Winning?

The Mayo Clinic staff addressed the pressure young athletes face in an article on the clinic's Web site.

> *Most young athletes can tell you that the competitive drive to win can be fierce. Besides the satisfaction of personal*

gain, young athletes often pursue dreams of a medal for their country, a college scholarship or a place on a professional team. In such an environment, the use of performance-enhancing drugs has become increasingly common.

For a growing number of athletes, winning at all costs includes taking performance-enhancing drugs. Some may appear to achieve physical gains from such drugs, but at what cost? The truth is, the long-term effects of performance-enhancing drugs haven't been rigorously studied. And short-term benefits are tempered by many drawbacks.

Take the time to learn about the benefits, risks and many unknowns regarding so-called performance-enhancing drugs. You may decide that the benefits aren't worth the risks.[1]

As a relatively recent phenomenon, there is a limit to the extent of thorough medical research on performance-enhancing drugs. Side effects are clearly known and

Swaying the Opinion

National Public Radio held a debate in front of a live audience in January 2008. The issue was whether steroid use should be accepted in sports.

Prior to the debate, a poll of audience members showed that 18 percent accepted the suggestion to tolerate performance-enhancing drug use in competitive sports, 63 percent opposed it, and 19 percent were undecided.

After listening to the debate, more audience members accepted the idea. By the end, 37 percent agreed with the idea, 59 percent opposed it, and 4 percent remained undecided.

medical experts have established clear areas of concern, but wide-ranging opinions remain on the extent of the actual danger.

Edward R. Laskowski, MD, of the President's Council on Physical Fitness in Sports, points out another uncertainty in the debate. Laskowski says proponents of the drugs can exaggerate the positive effects on performance. He said young athletes need to be aware that performance has more to do with skill and hard work than pills and sports drinks. Laskowski said there is reason for concern that young athletes will copy famous sports figures who use unproven substances in an effort to gain a competitive edge: "There's a danger that kids or young adults will think: 'If I want to be like that, I'll need to take something.' . . . There's a tendency to look for an external agent as a magic bullet, a magic pill that's going to help us perform better. The truth is there isn't any."[2]

In general, there are concerns that the dangers are more significant on growing and developing bodies. Some opponents of performance-enhancing drug use consider the influence Olympic and professional athletes have over youngsters as an added part of the concern on the issue.

Julian Savulescu, professor of practical ethics at the University of Oxford, takes the stance that limiting drugs in sports is unnecessary. Instead, he proposes concentration on protecting young athletes. "Our proposal is enforceable, it frees up the limited resources to focus on drugs that may be affecting children, which we grant should not have access to drugs," Savulescu said. "As we've argued, performance enhancement is not against the spirit of sport, it's been a part of sport through its whole history, and to be human is to be better, or at least try to be better."[4]

WHERE IS THE LINE?

In some arguments, the case is made against which types of substances an athlete can legally use. In other arguments, the question is not a matter of type, but of quantity.

Cases can be made for vitamins and supplements that are backed by research. Newer supplements can fall into gray areas. One example is androstenedione, which was legal until the Anabolic Steroid Control Act of 2004 made its use illegal without a prescription because it was determined to be a steroid precursor. Steroid precursors are substances that the body can convert into anabolic steroids.

Anabolic steroids are banned specifically by many sports organizations. The issue extends beyond rules of the game. Anabolic steroids are legal only when prescribed by a doctor for medical reasons. Merely obtaining the steroids without prescription can violate federal and state laws.

The most common performance-enhancing drug issues revolve around drugs intended to speed up the training process by building muscle more quickly or helping the body recover from the wear and tear of intense workouts. There

Reasons for Teen Use

An article authored by Mayo Clinic staff outlined the motivations that might push teen athletes toward using performance-enhancing drugs.

- **Frustration**
  Use may help athletes break a plateau in training.
- **Curiosity**
  Athletes want to see what could happen with their performance if they try drugs.
- **Psychological effects**
  Some performance-enhancing substances give a "high" feeling.
- **Peer pressure**
  Use may be accepted by others or athletes may feel pressured to keep up with opponents who are using.
- **Implicit approval**
  Adults may disregard signs of use.

High school student Christopher O'Sullivan appeared in court facing steroid use charges in March 2005.

are also other attempts to gain an edge. Caffeine and over-the-counter drugs used for other purposes can be misused as stimulants to try to boost energy for a competition. And in competitions where steadiness—rather than intensity—is at a premium, athletes may be tempted to take something to help remain calm.

The National Collegiate Athletic Association is one sports organization that places limits on caffeine levels, making it illegal for a competitive athlete to have too much in his or her system.

Why Is It a Problem?

If legal, the use of performance-enhancing drugs can be viewed as just one more step in the effort to improve performance. However, as an illegal act in most sports, it is viewed as cheating to gain an advantage. "The use of performance-enhancing drugs is not accidental; it is planned and deliberate with the sole objective of getting an unfair advantage," said Dick Pound, chairman of the World Anti-Doping Agency.[6]

There are wide differences of opinion on whether adult elite athletes truly need to be protected from the dangers of steroids and similar drugs. "I am not willing to pay the price for legalizing steroids and performance-enhancing drugs, because I've seen too often what it can do," sportscaster George Michael said during a National Public Radio debate on the issue. Michael went on to say:

> I don't want to go to the cemetery and tell all the athletes who are dead there, "Hey guys, soon you'll have a lot more of your friends coming, because we're going to legalize this stuff."[7]

"If something could be said to be natural, we tend to be OK with it. If it's lab-made or synthetic, we tend to be leery. But even synthetic drugs and man-made technology seem to be OK if the aim is to make sick people better or broken people whole again."[5]
—Radley Balko, senior editor and investigative journalist, Reason *magazine*

Norman Fost, professor of pediatrics and bioethics at the University of Wisconsin, was part of the same debate. He admitted to side effects but claimed that the other dangers have been exaggerated. Fost said:

> I ask you in the audience to quickly name, in your own minds, a single elite athlete who's had a stroke or heart attack while playing sports. It's hard to come up with one. Anabolic steroids do have undesirable side effects: acne, baldness, voice changes . . . infertility. But sport itself is far more dangerous, and we don't prohibit it. The number of deaths from playing professional football and college football are 50 to 100 times higher than even the wild exaggerations about steroids. More people have died playing baseball than have died of steroid use.[8]

Fost's statements highlight the lack of specific evidence around the use of these drugs. Steroid use is believed to cause side effects that could endanger or ultimately shorten one's life, but until more specific research is completed, exact numbers are difficult to pin down.

Robert Hazelton, a former heavyweight boxer and steroid user, claims he lost his legs because of steroid use.

The Drug Enforcement Administration engaged in an investigation of illicit steroid labs. This photo shows steroids that were confiscated.

STEROIDS, HORMONES, AND STIMULANTS

Athletes turn to stimulants, supplements, steroids, and human growth hormone (HGH) for a variety of reasons.

Performance potentially can be "enhanced" in many ways. Athletes may seek chemical help in making their training more effective or in helping fight off fatigue and soreness from workouts. They may look for a substance that can boost their performance in an actual game situation. The increased muscle, for some, creates a more impressive physical appearance.

Anabolic steroids remain the most publicized and controversial of the performance-enhancing drugs. "Hypothetically, there's a good chance that taking anabolic steroids will have a chance to make you faster and quicker," said Jay Hoffman, the chairman of the department of Health & Exercise Science at the College of New Jersey.[1] Hoffman said he took steroids during his days as a National Football League player.

Dr. Gary Wadler is a New York University School of Medicine professor who serves as a consultant to the U.S. Department of Justice on anabolic-androgenic steroid use. He warns of the extreme price athletes risk taking for those gains. "Although there are many types of steroids with varying degrees of anabolic and androgenic properties, it's the anabolic property of steroids that lures athletes," Wadler said. "They take them to primarily increase muscle mass and strength."[2]

Wadler said side effects are prevalent whether steroids are taken orally or injected: "The side effects associated for the oral form were discovered to be especially worrisome for the liver. . . . But the injectable steroids aren't free of side effects either. There is no free ride and there is a price to be paid with either form."[3]

SUPPLEMENTS AND STEROID PRECURSORS

Creatine is a supplement some athletes use to try to improve performance in sports that involve short bursts of intense activity. Creatine monohydrate is a naturally produced compound that releases energy to muscles. Creatine can also be ingested through meats and fish that are high in protein.

The supplement creatine is often used in amounts well over what manufacturers recommend. Researchers see it as a supplement that can lead to anabolic steroid use.

The transition from supplement to steroid is not limited to a conscious choice by an athlete. The U.S. government changed the way it looked at several items, previously considered supplements, with the passage of the Anabolic Steroid Control Act of 2004. Steroid precursors, which are used to increase

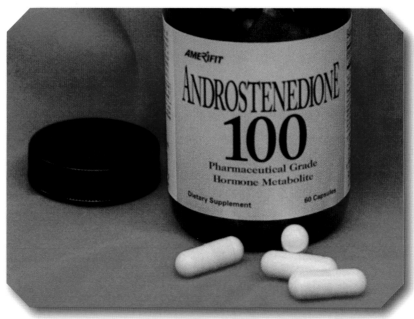

Androstenedione, a dietary supplement that was found in the locker of Mark McGwire, is a steroid precursor.

muscle mass, are substances that the body can convert into anabolic steroids. The act made most steroid precursors illegal without a prescription.

Androstenedione, Androstenediol, Norandrostenedione, and Norandrostenediol were among the steroid precursors that became prescription-only items. Dehydroepiandrosterone (DHEA) remains legally available as an over-the-counter supplement, but illegal in the rules of many sports organizations, including the Olympics.

ANABOLIC STEROIDS AND HGH

Testosterone is a naturally occurring male sex hormone. The most common anabolic steroids are synthetic forms of testosterone.

Steroids, which come in the form of injections, pills, and creams, have several legitimate medical uses. For example, testicular cancer often requires the removal of the testes in men. After surgery, these men are prescribed oral anabolic steroids to replace the testosterone that their bodies are no longer able to produce. After certain kinds of surgery, major body burns, and cancer, the patient

---

Legal in 1998

The drug androstenedione first became famous in 1998 when Associated Press reporter Steve Wilstein noticed it in the locker of St. Louis Cardinals slugger Mark McGwire.

McGwire was on his way to breaking one of Major League Baseball's most prestigious records when he hit 70 home runs to easily surpass the season total of 61 established by Roger Maris with the New York Yankees in 1961.

At the time, "andro" was viewed simply as a nutritional supplement. The federal government has since changed its position. The Food and Drug Administration determined the product to be a steroid precursor, posing the same risks as steroids, when it told manufacturers to stop producing andro in 2004.

"Anyone who takes these products in sufficient quantities to build muscle or improve performance is putting himself or herself at risk for serious long-term and potentially irreversible health consequences," FDA Commissioner Mark McClellan said. [4]

Medical studies indicated that andro raised testosterone levels to above normal. Concerns were cited about the potential for effects to be greater in children going through puberty.

---

experiences a loss of muscle tissue. Anabolic steroids can be used in such cases, with exercise and diet, to build up muscle tissue as part of the rehabilitation process.

Athletes use anabolic steroids in an effort to build muscle and increase endurance. Many athletes, however, use anabolic steroids in much greater dosages than those intended for medical treatments.

Stanozolol is an anabolic steroid that many Olympic athletes, including one-time world 100-meter dash record-holder Ben Johnson of Canada, have tested positive for using. It is popular among track-and-field athletes. Tetrahydrogestrinone (THG) was originally marketed as a dietary supplement that was beneficial to athletes. It was found to be a new chemical variation of an anabolic steroid designed to avoid detection in drug tests.

Millions of Users in the United States

About 3 million people illegally use anabolic steroids in the United States, according to the Mayo Clinic.

Of that amount, about one in four started as a teenager and one out of every ten is currently a teenager.

HGH, like anabolic steroids, is another drug some athletes use to try to improve muscle growth and recovery from workouts. Other hormones, such as darbepoetin and erythropoietin (EPO), are used to stimulate the production of red blood cells. Increased red blood cell production can boost an athlete's endurance and aerobic capacity.

Insulin, the natural hormone secreted by the pancreas, is used as a drug to regulate blood sugar in diabetes patients. Athletes have used it to try to increase the impact of steroids.

STIMULANTS

Ephedrine, pseudoephedrine, amphetamines, and methamphetamines are the stimulants most commonly linked to use in sports. Athletes seeking improved alertness and endurance may seek stimulants, which increase

Potential Side Effects

The potential side effects differ according to the type of performance-enhancing drug. The most common of the side effects for each include:

- Creatine: nausea, muscle cramps, stomach pain, and diarrhea; in high doses, kidney, liver, or heart problems
- Anabolic steroids and steroid precursors: mood swings, including depression and "roid rage"; stunted growth; baldness in males; deep voice and facial hair in females; heart and liver damage; impotence in males
- HGH: excessive growth of head, feet, and hands; heart problems; diabetes
- EPO: high blood pressure, heart attacks
- Stimulants: headache, nervousness, anxiety, irregular heartbeat, heart attacks, strokes

heart rate and blood pressure. Stimulants have also been used to control weight, but can cause anxiety, headaches, and other physical symptoms.

A racing heartbeat can reach dangerous levels. Danish cyclist Kurt Jensen collapsed and died of a heart attack from an amphetamine overdose during the 1960 Olympics. British cyclist Tommy Simpson died of heart failure, aggravated by amphetamines, during the 1967 Tour de France.

The use of stimulants predated many of the other performance-enhancing drugs, which evolved out of modern scientific advances. Ephedra, which contains ephedrine and pseudoephedrine, was marketed as a dietary supplement until it was banned by the Food and Drug Administration (FDA) in 2004. These easy-to-obtain, over-the-counter supplements promised

Commonly Associated Sports

Athletes who compete against each other often seek out the same performance-enhancing drugs because of the similar goals in their training methods.

The sports most commonly associated with several drugs include:

• Creatine: weightlifting, wrestling, sprinting
• Anabolic steroids: track and field, football, baseball, bodybuilding, weightlifting
• HGH: swimming, baseball, track and field
• Other hormones: cycling, distance running, cross-country skiing
• Stimulants: cycling, track and field, hockey

weight loss or increased energy, but came with a heavy price: irregular heartbeats, insomnia, and the potential for dependence. Manufacturers of ephedra-based products continue to wage legal battles against the ban.

Former Senator George Mitchell during a New York news conference in which he discussed his investigation of steroid use in baseball

Ken Caminiti, a former baseball star, died of a heart attack at a young age. He had admitted to steroid use.

Baseball's Issues Become Public

The federal investigation into activity at the Bay Area Laboratory Co-Operative (BALCO) did not end with the uncovering of connections to Barry Bonds. Major League Baseball (MLB) commissioner Bud Selig ordered an internal investigation into the use of steroids in baseball. After Bonds, Jason Giambi and Gary Sheffield were among the athletes called to testify in front of a grand jury.

Former Senator George Mitchell led a 21-month investigation culminating in a detailed report that he released in December of 2007. By the time the Mitchell Report was out, Bonds had a rival for the role of biggest baseball star to be linked to steroids. Among the many famous players now mentioned publicly as possible steroid users was Roger Clemens, a seven-time winner of the Cy Young Award as the best pitcher in his league.

INCREASING THE VOLUME

Like many other sports, baseball had been the subject of whispers in the past. The Mitchell Report helped bring many of the game's serious issues into public conversation.

Before players looked at ways of gaining power through performance-enhancing drugs, they sought a different type of edge. The 162-game schedule meant ballplayers competed virtually every day for six months. The season involved frequent airline travel and switching between day and night games.

These elements joined to give baseball players a set of challenges unique from other sports. The busy schedule combined with the game's slow pace made staying alert a priority long before players sought ways to artificially pump up their power. Amphetamines, known as "greenies" or "speed," have been prevalent in the game for decades. Players often took the pills for an energy boost prior to games.

As author of the baseball diary *Ball Four*, former MLB pitcher Jim Bouton gave fans an unprecedented and often scandalous

Greenies

While steroids receive the most attention, it is possible that MLB's 2006 decision to test players for amphetamines could have a larger impact than testing for steroids. Called "greenies" because of their color, these amphetamines were part of the game of baseball long before steroids.

"It's going to have a lot bigger effect on the game than steroid testing," Atlanta Braves all-star third baseman Chipper Jones said. "It's more rampant than steroids."[1]

MLB Commissioner Bud Selig informed MLB Players Association director Donald Fehr in a letter that it was his intent to erase all performance-enhancing drugs from baseball, not just steroids. Selig wrote: "It's time to put the whispers about amphetamine use to bed once and for all. . . . To the extent that our culture has tolerated the use of these substances, the culture must change."[2]

An athlete's first positive test for amphetamines leads to a series of random tests. A second positive test results in a 25-game suspension. A third positive test results in an 80-game suspension—almost half of a 162-game season. The fourth positive test is left to the commissioner to determine the punishment, including the possibility of a lifetime ban from baseball.

look inside the sport. This included an education about greenies. Bouton said he is not surprised that today's players would experiment with steroids to gain an edge:

> *How could I be surprised? In the 1970s, half of the guys in the big leagues were taking greenies, and if we had steroids, we would have taken those, too. I said in* Ball Four, *if there was a pill that could guarantee you would win 20 games but would take five years off your life, players would take it. The only thing I didn't know at the time was the name.*[3]

Bouton's assessment appears to be accurate. In 1998, during Mark McGwire's pursuit of the single-season home run record, andro was legal. In 2004, the U.S. Food and Drug Administration (FDA) ordered the production of products featuring androstenedione to cease. Androstenedione, originally marketed as a nutritional

Androstenedione Banned

On March 11, 2004, the U.S. FDA announced that it was sending warning letters to 23 companies asking them to cease distributing products sold as dietary supplements containing androstenedione. The companies were warned that they could face enforcement actions if they did not comply.

In explaining the action, the FDA stated that it "believes that these products may increase the risk of serious health problems because they are converted in the body to testosterone which is an androgenic and anabolic steroid."[4]

The National Collegiate Athletic Association (NCAA) and the National Football League (NFL), as well as the International Olympic Committee (IOC), had already banned androstenedione.

Several medical groups had cautioned against the use of steroids and their precursors because of potential side effects.

Mark McGwire hit 70 home runs during his 1998 baseball season.

supplement, was determined to be a steroid precursor. That meant that once it was ingested, the body would convert it into a steroid.

Steroid Era

Friends of Bonds have attributed his decision to use steroids to his realization that other players were compiling impressive home run numbers—and benefiting from the fame and financial rewards that went with those numbers—with the help of steroids.

The use of steroids in baseball appeared to be growing before Bonds was introduced to BALCO and its owner, Victor Conte.

In 2002, Ken Caminiti, who had retired from baseball the year before, told *Sports Illustrated* that the use of steroids had helped him win the 1996 National League Most Valuable Player award. Caminiti estimated that at the time at least half of his fellow MLB players were also using. He explained: "I've made a ton of mistakes. . . . I don't think using steroids is one of them."[5]

Caminiti died of a heart attack at age 41 on October 10, 2004. Medical examiners believe abuse of other drugs, including cocaine, painkillers, and alcohol, contributed to his heart condition.

By the time of Caminiti's death, BALCO had been raided. The number of names linked to the investigation of the San Francisco-area lab was growing.

Jose Canseco and Mark McGwire were once known as the "Bash Brothers" in their days as young slugging teammates with the Oakland Athletics. Both men were called to testify at a congressional hearing into steroid use in baseball on March 17, 2005. Canseco had recently released a book entitled

Rafael Palmeiro

Rafael Palmeiro was in the news throughout 2005. Palmeiro testified before Congress on March 17 that he had "never used steroids. Period."[6]

In July, he became the fourth player in MLB history to have at least 3,000 hits and 500 home runs in a career.

On August 1 of that same year, Palmeiro was suspended by baseball for testing positive for steroids.

Juiced: Wild Times, Rampant 'Roids, Smash Hits & How Baseball Got Big and was eager to talk about the issue. McGwire repeatedly told lawmakers that he was not there to talk about the past and referred to advice from his attorney when refusing to answer direct questions.

The perception after BALCO, Canseco's book, and the questions from Congress was that baseball needed to assess the influence of illegal drugs in the sport. The Mitchell Report was Selig's answer to that need, and another investigation began, calling even more big-name players to the spotlight in the years to come. Baseball as an organization was now participating officially in producing the claims against its players.

MITCHELL REPORT AFTERMATH

Clemens was named in the Mitchell Report along with Andy

Pettitte, a fellow pitcher and teammate on the New York Yankees and Houston Astros. The reaction of the two teammates, who are close friends, became the most followed story in the months after the release of the Mitchell Report. Pettitte acknowledged some of what investigators found and admitted to limited usage of steroids. Clemens vigorously proclaimed his innocence.

Clemens and Brian McNamee, his former trainer, told vastly different stories when they appeared before the House Committee on Oversight and Government Reform in another hearing about steroids in baseball on February 13, 2008.

McNamee told the committee that he injected Clemens with steroids and other performance-enhancing drugs. Clemens said the injections contained only vitamins.

Committee chairman Henry Waxman, a Democrat from California, summed up the differences in the testimony, which was given when both men were under oath:

> Someone isn't telling the truth. If Mr. McNamee is lying, then he has acted inexcusably and he has made Mr. Clemens an innocent victim. If Mr. Clemens isn't telling the truth, then

he has acted shamefully and he has smeared Mr. McNamee.
I don't think there is anything in between.[7]

The names included in the Mitchell Report
spanned many MLB teams. Whether the player
named confirmed suspicions of use or denied the
accusations, public trust had been violated as fingers
were pointed and many questions went unanswered.

Teammates Andy Pettitte, left, and Roger Clemens, right, were both named in the Mitchell Report.

Canadian sprinter Ben Johnson was the center of media attention when his medals were stripped after the 1988 Summer Olympics.

INDIVIDUAL SPORTS

Track and field is a sport that often falls into the background during non-Olympic years. Every four years, however, the attention returns to the sport, as it becomes the centerpiece of the Summer Olympics.

Certain track-and-field events traditionally draw more attention than others. The 100-meter dash has a level of prestige that is unmatched. The unofficial title of world's fastest man—or woman—is generally reserved for either the reigning 100-meter Olympic champion or the 100-meter world-record holder. When the same person fits both descriptions, there is little room for debate.

Canada's Ben Johnson held the distinction as world's fastest man for all of two days in 1988. He was both Olympic champion and world-record holder as the result of a special race in front of 80,000 fans in Seoul, South Korea, on September 24 of that year.

The title was claimed in a showdown with one of track and field's all-time greats, Carl Lewis of the United States. Few moments in the sport's history rivaled Johnson's race with Lewis. Few moments have created as much lasting controversy or have done more to tarnish one man's image.

Lewis ultimately won ten Olympic medals—nine gold and one silver—in his career. Included in that list is the 1984 gold in the 100-meter dash, when Johnson had to settle for the second-place silver medal.

Between the 1984 and 1988 Olympic 100-meter showdowns, Lewis and Johnson had beaten each other in different races. Johnson's victories over Lewis included a world record 9.93 seconds in the 1987 World Championships in Rome.

When Johnson burst from the starting blocks in the 1988 Olympics and left Lewis behind, he was about to become the fastest man in the world. No one had ever beaten the 9.79-second time that he posted. Johnson looked over his shoulder to check on Lewis and started celebrating as he crossed the finish line, leading observers to believe he could have shaved a few more hundredths of a second off his time if not for the minor distractions. Immortality awaited Johnson. But his effort went down in history for reasons other than skill.

Two days later, the International Olympic Committee (IOC) announced that Johnson's urine had been tested after the race and it showed traces of an anabolic steroid. Because anabolic steroids were illegal for Olympic athletes, Johnson's 100-meter title was taken away and his records were erased.

"Looking back and knowing what we know now about the extent of drug use in sport, our shock at Johnson's downfall seems painfully naïve."[1]
—David Belton, British Broadcasting Company (BBC) correspondent, in 2001

Lewis went in the books as the winner in a time of 9.92 that became the new world record.

JOHNSON'S RESPONSE

Johnson immediately denied using steroids and said a drink he took before the race must have been spiked. He repeatedly said he had "never ever knowingly" used a banned substance.[2] The following year, however, Johnson admitted during a Canadian judicial inquiry that he had been taking pills and injections for seven years.

Johnson explained that drug use was widespread and he did what was necessary to keep others from gaining an advantage. His explanation has varied through the years, including renewed accusations that he was set up. Although he admitted using performance-enhancing drugs, Johnson pointed the finger at his rival, Lewis, as possibly having something to do with failing the drug test. Johnson's name is not found in official records.

Johnson's Punishment

Canadian sprinter Ben Johnson was banned from competing for two years and lost his Olympic medals and world records when he tested positive for an anabolic steroid at the 1988 Olympics in South Korea.

He attempted a comeback, but after testing positive for steroids again in 1993, Johnson was banned from competition for life by the International Association of Athletics Federations.

There was also a monetary price to Johnson's infamy. "I lost 100 million [dollars] in endorsements," Johnson said.[3]

In some ways, it is as if the 9.79 sprint to glory in front of 80,000 spectators never happened. "In the eyes of the people, I'm still the best sprinter of all time," Johnson said in a 2005 interview.[4]

Johnson often points out that he was not alone in seeking an edge. Others in the Olympic final that night in Seoul tested positive for drugs at some point in their careers.

Johnson claims that Lewis also should be on the list of athletes who failed drug tests, but that the U.S. Olympic Committee covered up positive tests. Published reports in 2003, citing information revealed by Dr. Wade Exum, a disgruntled former U.S. anti-doping official, indicated that Lewis tested positive for a banned stimulant at the 1988 U.S. Olympic trials, but was still allowed to be part of the team in Seoul. "He tested positive," Johnson said. "They all tested positive. They're all doin' something. Everybody's got dirt in them."[5]

BEATING THE CLOCK

Johnson may have been the first North American athlete with such a high profile to be taken down in view of the world sporting community. He was not alone, however, in his troubles.

Athletes who are racing the clock and other measurements of success are no different from those who compete directly against other athletes. Olympic sports and other individual competitions, such as cycling, swimming, and weightlifting, have joined track and field in developing their share of controversy. Some of the earliest hints of steroid use at the Olympic Games came in swimming.

East German women dominated the first swimming World Championships in 1973. They won all but two individual events, and eight of the swimmers posted record times. Drug testing was not conducted until the 1976 Olympics in Montreal, but even without tests, suspicions arose about the East German team.

In 1991, 20 coaches from East Germany released a joint statement, admitting what had been suspected: that they were administering anabolic steroids to some of their swimmers. The coaches wrote, "We confirm that anabolic steroids were used in former East German swimming. . . . Not all of us were involved in doping. The extent varied."[6] It took another 15 years, but the German government, the German Olympic Sports Union, and the pharmaceutical company Jenapharm eventually compensated 167 former East German athletes because of health problems they developed following the steroid use.

China rose to prominence in women's swimming in the mid-1990s, winning 12 of 16 events at the World Championships in Rome, Italy, in 1994. Soon, however, the Chinese women swimmers were the leaders in a new category: failed drug tests, including seven at the Asian Games in Japan.

Irish swimmer Michelle Smith was under suspicion after winning three golds and a silver medal at the 1996 Olympics in Atlanta, Georgia. Smith made rapid improvements in her times after beginning to train with her husband, Erik de Bruin, who was under suspension as a discus thrower because of a failed drug test. Smith acknowledged the suspicions, but pointed to the drug tests she had passed and gave another explanation for her improvement. "I train six days a week, six hours a day," she said. "I eat, sleep and train. This is the culmination of all that work."[7] When Smith was caught trying to tamper with one of her drug samples in 1998, she was suspended for four years.

A cyclist sits down in protest of the media's focus on performance-enhancing drug use during the 1998 Tour de France.

The sport of cycling's premier event, the Tour de France, has been surrounded by drug scandals for years. The Tour de France has suspended cyclists and former champions who have been accused of cheating. The 1998 race was interrupted during a police investigation into drugs and a protest by competitors about the investigation. The event reached new levels in 2006 when, for the first time, it stripped a champion of his title when U.S. athlete Floyd Landis tested positive for high levels of synthetic testosterone. In a statement, Landis declared: "I have never taken any banned substance. . . . I was the strongest man at the Tour de France, and that is why I am the champion."[8]

Landis fought the penalty but the decision was not overturned.

Back in the News

Olympic champion Marion Jones was among the track and field athletes implicated in the 2003 investigation of the Bay Area Laboratory Co-Operative (BALCO). Jones was called to testify along with baseball stars Barry Bonds, Jason Giambi, and Gary Sheffield.

The one-time World's Fastest Woman now joined the former World's Fastest Man in being sidelined by problems with performance-enhancing drugs. Jones admitted using "the Clear," one of BALCO's steroid products, for approximately two years beginning in 1999, when coach Trevor Graham first gave it to her.

After years of denying allegations of steroid use, Jones also pleaded guilty in 2007 to lying to federal investigators in two cases, one involving performance-enhancing drugs and the other a related check-fraud scheme. Jones then stepped outside the White Plains, New York, courthouse and made a public apology.

> *It's with a great amount of shame that I stand before you and tell you that I have betrayed your trust.*
>
> *I have been dishonest, and you have the right to be angry with me. I have let (my family)*

Paying the Price

Marion Jones lost a 2001 World Championships medal when Kelli White, one of her relay teammates, admitted three years later to doping.

Jones admitted that she had used steroids when training for the 2000 Olympics. The women who ran with her on two relay teams lost their medals as part of the punishment for Jones's actions.

The International Olympic Committee (IOC) disqualified the athletes on the winning 1,600-meter relay team and the team that had taken second in the 400-meter relay. The IOC also ordered the U.S. Olympic Committee (USOC) to take back the medals given to 1,600-meter relay members and 400-meter relay team members.

Jones returned her medals after her admission in 2007. USOC chief executive officer Jim Scherr said the decision "illustrates just how far-reaching the consequences of doping can be. When an athlete makes the choice to cheat, others end up paying the price, including teammates, competitors and fans."[9]

down. I have let my country down, and I have let myself down. I recognize that by saying I'm deeply sorry, it might not be enough and sufficient to address the pain and hurt that I've caused you.

Therefore, I want to ask your forgiveness for my actions, and I hope you can find it in your heart to forgive me.[10]

Jones, who won five medals at the 2000 Olympic Games in Sydney, Australia, had been questioned about her knowledge of the involvement of Tim Montgomery in the check-fraud scheme. Montgomery was Jones's former boyfriend and another elite U.S. sprinter.

Jones reported to federal prison in Fort Worth, Texas, on March 7, 2008, to serve six months. She was sentenced to that amount of time for lying under oath about performance-enhancing drugs and, at the same time, was serving a two-month sentence for lying about the check scheme. She was also sentenced to 400 hours of community service.

Record Erased

U.S. sprinter Tim Montgomery set a world record in the 100-meter dash with a time of 9.78 seconds in Paris, France, on September 14, 2002.

But Montgomery's drug use was discovered. When Montgomery was banned from track and field for two years in 2005, part of his punishment included five years' worth of his records being disqualified. Although his record had since been broken, the ruling treats the issue as if Montgomery never held the world record.

Montgomery was then banned from the sport in the aftermath of the investigation into BALCO.

U.S. sprinter Marion Jones celebrates as she crosses the finish line
to win a gold medal at the 2000 Sydney Olympic Games.

Steve Courson, a former NFL offensive lineman, testified during a House Committee hearing in April 2005.

POWER SOURCE

hroughout the history of sports, players keep getting bigger and stronger. In 2005, former National Football League (NFL) player Steve Courson told a congressional committee that drastic steps are needed to reverse the trend in which more than 300 professional linemen were believed to weigh more than 300 pounds (136 kg) each.

"The lines of scrimmage are bigger than ever," Courson said. "The league might consider a weight limit. Anyone with severe body weight is facing serious consequences, especially if they don't lose weight after they retire."[1]

Courson said that he used steroids throughout his career to reach the size and strength necessary to be competitive in the league. The NFL, compared to other sports, has a history of thorough drug testing, which catches a few players using illegal performance-enhancing drugs but has not revealed widespread usage. Courson told Congress that research was needed "to clean up the loopholes in drug testing."[2]

Part of steroid use by athletes who know they face tests is the use of "masking agents" that make the steroids difficult to detect in tests. Courson said he witnessed "a lot of use" as an NFL player from 1978 to 1985 before the testing program went into effect in 1987.[3] He said he believes the serious heart problems he faces stem from the steroid use.

Then-NFL Commissioner Paul Tagliabue said he believed the testing program works. He said that

III players had tested positive since 1989 with 54 receiving four-game suspensions and 57 choosing to retire. Only two of the 54 who were suspended tested positive a second time.

DOUBLE STANDARD

The "Steroid Era" in baseball is marked by an increase in home-run hitters and a notable difference in the size of players. Football has long been played by huge men, but in many ways, the sport has avoided some of the scrutiny baseball faces.

Wallace Matthews, a sports columnist for *Newsday*, a Long Island, New York, newspaper, noted the discrepancy as the government looked closely again at baseball in the 2008 hearings, following the release of the Mitchell Report in December of 2007. He compared the reactions to accusations made against New York Yankees pitcher Roger Clemens with a suspension for a failed drug test by San Diego Chargers linebacker Shawne Merriman. Matthews wrote:

Merriman Suspension

Shawne Merriman was the NFL's Defensive Rookie of the Year in 2005. He was also a starter for the American Football Conference team in the Pro Bowl after the season.

The San Diego Chargers linebacker tested positive for steroids and received a four-game suspension from the league. Merriman wound up sitting out one-quarter of the 2006 season.

When Roger Clemens becomes eligible for baseball's Hall of Fame, the most intense debate over his qualifications will have nothing to do with his 354 victories, or seven Cy Young Awards or his 4,672 strikeouts.

It will have everything to do with the allegations of HGH use made in the Mitchell Report and repeated—many would say, confirmed—by his accuser, Brian McNamee, in sworn testimony before a congressional committee.

When the time comes for Shawne Merriman to be considered for induction into the Pro Football Hall of Fame, the matter of his positive test for the anabolic steroid nandrolone probably won't even come up in the discussion.

. . . While the mere allegation of steroid or HGH use gets a ballplayer a miserable day in Washington, football players who actually test positive—something neither Clemens nor Andy Pettitte has—get a four-week vacation followed by a leaguewide campaign of rehabilitation.

And in Hollywood, juicing up gets you nothing but a multimillion-dollar contract to do action movies in your [sixties].

So when [Yankees owner Hank] Steinbrenner expresses frustration over the intensity with which Congress has gone after baseball players, while holding the NFL up as some paragon of drug-free virtue, he has a point. [4]

Matthews is not suggesting the rules be loosened in Major League Baseball, but instead, that the rules be tightened up in football: "If you're going to clean up one house in the neighborhood, you better clean up them all."[5]

Emphasis on Strength

The extreme emphasis on size creates an intense pressure on some athletes. When power matches power in direct physical battles, an athlete needs to be able to match his opponent's force to succeed.

This issue may have first been visible in Olympic weightlifting. Football and the sports/entertainment world of professional wrestling have also had a history of high-profile cases related to drug use.

Former baseball Most Valuable Player (MVP) Ken Caminiti, who died at age 41, is not the only casualty. Football and professional wrestling athletes have also had high-profile deaths linked to steroids.

Like Caminiti, football star Lyle Alzado told his story to *Sports Illustrated*, raising awareness of steroid use, before his death. Alzado was a two-time All-Pro and a Super Bowl champion in a 15-year career as a defensive lineman for the Denver Broncos, the Cleveland Browns, and the Los Angeles Raiders.

Lyle Alzado died in 1992.

He died at age 43 from brain cancer. Although a medical link has not been established, Alzado went public with statements that he believed his heavy use of anabolic steroids caused the rare cancer.

Alzado was not recruited out of high school and was turned down by a junior college. Alzado said the discovery of steroids helped turn him into a feared player at Yankton College, a small South Dakota school that was not part of the National Collegiate Athletic Association. The Denver Broncos stumbled across film of Alzado and made him their fourth pick in the 1971 NFL draft. This created an opportunity for him to make an impact.

"My first year with the Broncos, I was like a maniac," Alzado said. "I outran, outhit, outanythinged everybody. All along I was taking steroids and I saw they made me play better and better."[6]

Alzado made a lasting impression on the game, earning awards as the American Football Conference Defensive Player of the Year in 1977 and as the NFL Comeback Player of the Year in 1982. He received attention in other ways, too. The NFL wrote strict rules against helmet throwing after Alzado ripped the helmet off New York Jets tackle Chris Ward and threw it. "The guy had a split personality," Raiders teammate Greg Townsend said. "On the field, he had this tough image that he projected. Off the field he was the gentle giant."[7]

Alzado parlayed his fame into roles in 15 movies. He also acknowledged his use of steroids. The year before his death, he appeared on the cover of *Sports Illustrated,* when he wrote a first-person story about his steroid use. "It was addicting, mentally addicting," Alzado wrote. "I just didn't feel strong unless I was taking something."[8] Despite Alzado's beliefs, there is no way to prove his steroid use was related to his death.

There was also speculation about the role steroids may have played in the death of professional wrestler Chris Benoit, but for entirely different reasons. The bodies of Benoit, his wife, and seven-year-old son were found June 25, 2007, in their Fayetteville, Georgia, home. Investigations revealed that Benoit murdered his wife

A Troubling History

World Wrestling Entertainment (WWE) issued a statement regarding the deaths of Chris Benoit and his family. The WWE disputed speculation that steroids were involved in the 2007 murder-suicide in which the wrestler killed his wife and son before taking his own life.

The Benoit case continued a troubling history for professional wrestling. An ESPN article described six other prominent performers who had died between 1997 and 2005:

- Brian Pillman, 35, had a history of abusing steroids and died of a heart attack in 1997.
- Rick Rude, 40, died of heart failure believed to be caused by a steroid and drug overdose in 1999.
- Owen Hart, 34, died in an accidental fall that was part of a stunt in 1999.
- David Smith, 39, died of a heart attack in 2002, and his autopsy indicated that steroid use may have been to blame.
- Curt Hennig, 44, died of acute cocaine intoxication in 2003. His father claimed that steroids also played a role in his death.
- Eddie Guerrero, 38, died of heart failure in 2005. Earlier use of drugs and alcohol may have been a factor.

and son and then killed himself. Steroids were found in the home and the medical examiner determined that there were steroids in Benoit's body at the time. This raised the question of whether psychological side effects, such as "roid rage," could have been involved.

The Drug Enforcement Administration later revealed that Dr. Phil Astin had prescribed a ten-month supply of anabolic steroids for Benoit every three to four weeks in the year preceding the incident.

RAGING AGAINST A TEAMMATE

NFL linebacker Bill Romanowski is another athlete who was tied to the Bay Area Laboratory Co-Operative (BALCO) investigation. He agreed to pay damages to a former teammate after a fight that ended the player's career.

Romanowski ended a 16-year career in 2003. He tested positive for the steroid tetrahydrogestrinone (THG) in his final season. During a practice drill that year with the Oakland Raiders, Romanowski tore the helmet off Marcus Williams and punched him, breaking Williams' eye socket. Romanowski later agreed to compensate Williams $415,000. Following his career, Romanowski admitted to two years of steroid use before his failed drug test.

EVALUATING THE TESTS

The NFL has a year-round testing program that involves every player at some point. There are periodic off-season tests and players from each team are tested at random each week of the regular season and playoffs. "We do have one of the most comprehensive treatment and testing programs in all of sports," NFL spokesman Brian McCarthy said. "We work with the medical community to come up with state-of-the-art tests, not only testing, but discipline and education."[9]

Still, the congressional committee found in 2005 that the rumors and stories of rampant steroid use did not match with what the tests were finding. The NFL claimed that information from insiders told that more players were obtaining and using steroids than the number who actually tested positive. Robert White,

Adjusting the Tests

The NFL and the NFL Players Association reached an agreement in January of 2007 to strengthen testing programs and add erythropoietin (EPO) to the list of banned substances.

The number of players from each team to be tested each week on a random basis was increased from seven to ten.

The NFL announced it would continue to study the human growth hormone (HGH), as it was on the league's banned list. However, the NFL did not have an accurate test to determine its use.

a spokesman for committee chairman Thomas M. Davis III, a Republican from Virginia, noted the questions raised by the discrepancies. White said, "Does that raise the issue of whether there are ways around the tests? . . . That is obviously an inquiry we'll get into."[10]

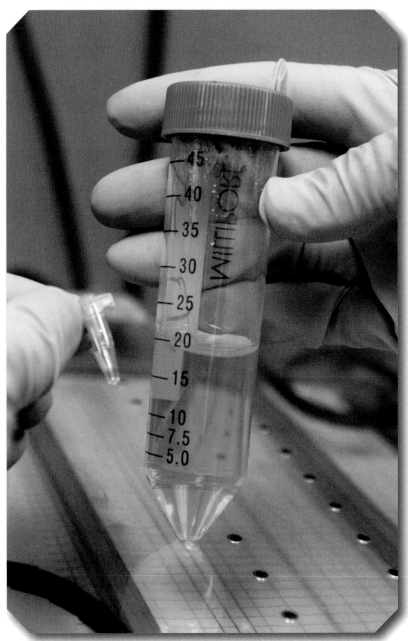

A urine sample tested at UCLA Olympic Analytical Laboratory

Don Hooton is an advocate for steroid testing in high schools.

YOUTHFUL CONCERNS

On more than one occasion, Don Hooton
has addressed large groups of strangers
to share memories of his son, Taylor Hooton.
Memories are all Don Hooton has left of Taylor.

He blames steroids—and pressure placed on young athletes—for that. Taylor Hooton took his life on July 15, 2003. Taylor was 17, in the summer between his junior and senior years of high school, when he died. Taylor seemed to have a happy teen life. He had the SAT scores he needed for college. He told his family that he had met the girl of his dreams. He expected to be a starting pitcher on his Plano West High School baseball team in Texas as a senior.

Taylor's popularity and the shock caused by his death were among the reasons that thousands attended his funeral. One of the many times that Don Hooton has told Taylor's story was during a 2004 Senate Drug Caucus just days from the first anniversary of his son's death. Hooton told the Senate:

> *Why would such a nice young man with his whole life in front of him take such an irrational step? I am convinced that anabolic steroids played a significant role in causing the severe depression that resulted in his suicide. Yes, steroids [are] a drug that I have learned can be just as lethal as any of the other "classical" drugs that we've heard so much about—heroin, cocaine, and others. And, . . . the events leading*

up to and including [Taylor's] suicide—are right out of the "textbook" on steroids.[1]

Hooton has become educated about steroids since his son's death. He makes a point of sharing what he has learned with anyone who will listen, particularly those who could head down the same path as his son.

Among the issues that trouble Hooton is advice that Taylor, at 6-foot-3 (1.91 m) and 175 pounds (79.4 kg), received from a high school junior varsity coach. Hooton said his son was told he needed to get bigger in order to improve his chances on the varsity team. Hooton says it was not necessary and that the coach never told Taylor how to accomplish this goal. "Senators, I've been around baseball all my life, and I still haven't figured out why he needed to be any 'bigger' in order to throw a baseball," Hooton said.[2]

Taylor Hooton found access to anabolic steroids. He gained 30 pounds (13.6 kg), but went through extreme mood swings from anger to depression.

"The reason that I am here today to share with you a little of what I've learned about steroids [is] so that you will be able to benefit from our experience. I am absolutely committed to seeing that Taylor's death will not go in vain."[3]

—Don Hooton, father of Taylor Hooton, who committed suicide after beginning a steroid-use regimen

Education Needed

The potential gains from performance-enhancing drugs are often visible before potential problems. Whether it is their intent, professional athletes who succeed with the help of steroids, human growth hormone (HGH), and other substances become role models for young athletes looking to make similar breakthroughs. "I kind of wince when I hear them say they're not role models," pediatric surgeon and sports

---

Doing Research

Following the suicide of his son, Taylor Hooton, Don Hooton set out to learn as much as he could about anabolic steroids. This included how and why his son used them.

Hooton read whatever he could find on the subject and talked to as many experts as he could. He gathered the information and presented it in speeches and presentations, including before a Senate committee.

Hooton told the Senate committee that most experts he had spoken with put the usage rate among high school students at 4 to 5 percent. The Texas resident said the usage rate was believed to be higher among male students in some parts of the country, including the South, and among athletes who were more likely to be enticed to use the drugs to build strength for a competitive edge.

Hooton told a Senate committee:

Let's not kid ourselves—our kids use steroids because they work well. They help the boys bulk up and give them the feeling that they are better in their particular sport than those players that are not taking steroids. And, once some of their teammates start using steroids, other members of the team feel the need to use the drug in order to remain competitive.[5]

A Leader in Research

Linn Goldberg serves as Professor of Medicine, Head of the Division of Health Promotion & Sports Medicine, Director of the Human Performance Laboratory, and Director of the Center for Health Promotion Research at the Oregon Health & Science University.

Goldberg has been awarded 30 research grants, with more than $26 million in funding, as principal or coinvestigator. He was the principal investigator for the Athletes Training and Learning to Avoid Steroids (ATLAS) program for male high school students.

Goldberg has been a featured speaker at international conferences and an expert witness in federal government hearings regarding performance-enhancing drug use among children, adolescents, and professional athletes.

medicine physician Marc Cardelia said.[4]

In some cases, supplements that were originally legal have, after additional research, been determined to be illegal products. The potential is there for even currently legal dietary supplements to be dangerous or a stepping stone to other drugs. "Those who start out using these supplements often end up moving on to harder drugs," Doctor Linn Goldberg said.[6]

Studies by the Centers for Disease Control and Prevention estimated that 1 in 45 high school students admitted using steroids in 1993, and that number was up to 1 out of every 16 in 2003.

Even those who support the premise of letting adult and professional athletes use performance-enhancing drugs generally agree that the associated risks are higher in teens. Cardelia stated, "They're a lot like other illicit drugs. They're habit forming, and there are signs of withdrawal when they come off, and behavioral changes associated with this."[7]

ATTACKING THE SITUATION

Goldberg and Hooton are among the leaders in educating those involved in high school sports about the dangers of performance-enhancing drugs. In addition to telling his story to major media outlets, speaking to high school students, and bringing the cause to the government, Hooton is raising money in his son's name to continue the fight.

During his appearance in Washington DC, Hooton said:

> To help fill this education void, we have just formed a non-profit foundation—The Taylor Hooton Foundation for Fighting Steroid Abuse. As far as we know, we are the only private group in existence that is organizing to help fight this battle. We have opened a Web site, and have begun a fund-raising campaign targeted at raising $5 million this year for this national education effort.[8]

On the same front, Goldberg and his colleague, Dr. Diane Elliott, with the Oregon Health & Science

ATLAS and ATHENA

ATLAS and ATHENA are educational programs that started in the 1990s and expanded during the first decade of the new millennium.

The programs use a coach and selected students, called "Squad Leaders," to educate others on issues involving the dangers of both performance-enhancing and recreational drugs. The program material is scripted and involves eight 45-minute sessions. Leaders provide a majority of instruction for their small group of teammates.

University, developed ATLAS in 1993 and ATHENA in 1997.

ATLAS stands for Athletes Training and Learning to Avoid Steroids and is geared toward male athletes. ATHENA stands for Athletes Targeting Healthy Exercise and Nutrition Alternatives and is geared toward issues specific to females. Both programs aspire to spread the word from student to student to help educate high school athletes about the dangers of both performance-enhancing and recreational drugs and substances, including alcohol.

The program took a step forward in 2007 when it gained the backing of the National Football League (NFL) and its Youth Football Fund, allowing the ATLAS and ATHENA programs to reach student athletes throughout the nation. ⌐

The Washington Redskins have partnered with Dr. Linn Goldberg, developer of ATLAS and ATHENA programs for athletes.

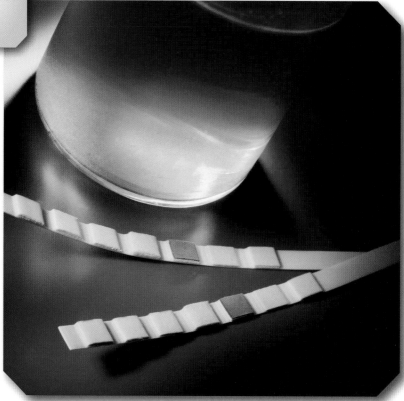

Some people have questioned the validity of drug tests, saying they often fail to catch those who are guilty of using performance-enhancing drugs.

DRUG TESTING

One of the most intense races in sports does not take place on a track or on a playing field, but in the laboratory.

Drug testers for sports organizations often find themselves trying to rally from behind in the competition with the "cheaters" they are trying to catch. In some cases, cheating is intentional. This applies to those who promote the use of illegal performance-enhancing drugs and take measures to develop "masking agents" that will disguise steroids and other chemicals. In other cases, scientists walk the fine lines of legality. This applies to those who develop supplements that will have steroidlike effects without technically being viewed as steroids. Those who test samples from players must work twice as hard to look for steroids in disguise.

It is unlikely that sports ethics will change and allow performance-enhancing drugs. But it is likely that the laboratory will continue to battle the rules and procedures, changing as each side tries to stay ahead of the other.

Testing Programs

The International Olympic Committee (IOC) and major sports leagues constantly update their drug-testing programs to try to keep up with advances in science. Lists of banned substances in international competition are updated each year.

The National Football League (NFL) adjusted its list of banned substances again in 2007. Major

League Baseball (MLB) did so in 2008 in the aftermath of the Mitchell Report on drug use in athletics. Both leagues worked out new deals with their players' unions.

Escalating Penalties

The NFL suspends players for four games with their first positive drug test. After a second failed drug test, a player is suspended for an entire year.

"It is important that the NFL and its players continue to be leaders on the issue of illegal and dangerous performance-enhancing drugs in sports," NFL commissioner Roger Goodell said in a statement released when the new policy was announced. "These latest improvements will help ensure that we continue to have a strong and effective program. . . . We will review and modify the policy on an ongoing basis."[1]

The NFL increased the number of players undergoing random tests each week, added tests for erythropoietin (EPO), and continued to pursue ways to test for Human Growth Hormone (HGH). EPO is a stimulant more commonly associated with endurance sports, but the NFL decided to test for it along with testing to detect low levels of testosterone. Previously, testosterone levels were only checked when confirming positive drug tests.

Gary Wadler, a physician and member of the World Anti-Doping Agency's prohibited substances committee, said adjusting the rules is not the most important issue. Wadler said the NFL needs to turn over control of testing its players to an external testing agency: "They cannot keep up with the science. That's not their business. Their business is putting on great championships."[2]

The NFL attempted to make its year-round testing program less predictable. The NFL also increased penalties to include making players refund portions of their signing bonuses for violations.

As the 2008 season was beginning, MLB struck a deal with the MLB Players Association to have more frequent testing in exchange for forgiveness of past transgressions by players named in the Mitchell Report. The changes also turned over more control of the testing process to the program's outside administrator. The changes were the third overhaul to the performance-enhancing drug testing program that was first introduced by the league in 2002.

"We are gratified that commissioner [Bud] Selig chose to accept [Senator] Mitchell's recommendation that no further punishment of players is warranted. In many instances the naming of players was punishment enough; in others it may have been unfair."[3]

—Donald Fehr, Major League Baseball Players Association executive director

MLB agreed not to name accused players publicly, as did the Mitchell Report, before they were given an opportunity to respond to allegations. The final result of the Mitchell Report was public discussion and some embarrassment for players, but no punishment from the league. Baseball commissioner Bud Selig stated, "It's time for the game to move forward. There is little to be gained at this point in debating dated misconduct and enduring numerous disciplinary proceedings."[4]

Wadler was again critical that testing responsibilities were not turned over to an entity such as the U.S. Anti-Doping

---

Cleaning Up Management

Players were not the only ones MLB needed to address in the aftermath of the Mitchell Report, an investigation into performance-enhancing drug use in the sport. The report revealed that there was a disturbingly complicated web of involvement that reached up the chain of command all the way to club managers.

Following the investigation, MLB accepted the Mitchell Report recommendation that it create certification standards for strength and conditioning coaches. Fingers were pointed not only at the athletes themselves but also at the management teams. It has been suspected that the upper managers of MLB teams were well aware of the use of performance-enhancing drugs by their players, but turned their heads the other way and allowed it to go on.

Commissioner Bud Selig was left to decide whether to impose any discipline on management employees who may have played a role in illegal drug use. Selig said that any fines that might be imposed would be donated to the Partnership for a Drug-Free America and the Taylor Hooton Foundation.

Agency. "It's another incremental step," he said. "It's better than it was but it's not where it needs to be."[5]

Making Adjustments

New products complicate the drug-testing issue. One of the Bay Area Laboratory Co-Operative (BALCO) contributions to the equation was tetrahydrogestrinone (THG), a steroid that was undetectable until a source provided antidoping officials with a sample for analysis. THG was linked to Modafinil, a prescription drug used to fight sleep disorders. Athletes were apparently using the stimulant to mask the properties of THG.

Along with prescription drugs, many nutritional supplements and dietary aids bring about confusion, whether intentional or unintentional, when they are brought on the market. San Diego Chargers linebacker Shawne Merriman joined many athletes from other sports when he insisted that his failed NFL test for nandrolone was the result of taking it unknowingly because it was in a supplement he was taking. Such a defense,

Designer Drugs

Tetrahydrogestrinone (THG) is known as a "designer drug." Designer drugs are drugs that are created in reaction to existing testing procedures. They are designed to be undetectable in drug tests.

whether sincere or insincere, is not usually accepted because leagues and governing bodies hold athletes responsible for knowing all products they are taking.

Why Bother?

Drug testing's intent is to eliminate unfair advantages that are deemed to be cheating by a sport's governing body. Evidence exists, however, that the tests often come up short of this goal.

Sports history is filled with examples of athletes who passed drug tests, performed successfully, eventually failed a drug test, denied using, and ultimately admitted a pattern of use. Sports researcher Lincoln Allison argues that athletes who are good at circumventing the rules are not getting caught: "The most pressing arguments for abandoning the present policy are that it doesn't work and probably catches the (relatively) innocent more than the guilty."[6]

Expensive, and arguably intrusive, testing often does fail to catch performance-enhancing drug users. Allison is not alone in the argument that testing may not be worth the trouble.

U.S. cyclist Lance Armstrong pointed out the frustration of being unable to fend off rumors of

Lance Armstrong won the Tour de France seven years in a row.

drug use while winning seven Tour de France titles.
Armstrong passed all drug tests, but skepticism
remained because of other instances of drug tests
failing to catch cheaters. "I'm not saying my best
defense is I've never tested positive," Armstrong
said.[7]

San Francisco Chronicle sports columnist Gwen
Knapp summarized why drug testing is not always the
answer when cyclists Jan Ullrich and Ivan Basso were

benched by their team for the 2006 Tour de France while being investigated by police.

> *Jan Ullrich and Ivan Basso never failed a drug test.*
>
> *Jason Grimsley never failed a drug test.*
>
> *The East Germans. World time-trial cycling champ David Millar. Yuan Yuan, the Chinese swimmer whose luggage for the 1998 World Championships contained 13 vials of human growth hormone.*
>
> *Never failed a drug test.*
>
> *. . . "Never failed a drug test" is virtually meaningless.*
>
> *When Congressional pressure forced baseball to dramatically increase penalties for failed drug tests last year, trumpets went off on Capitol Hill, naïvely declaring a major victory. Drug testing alone can't effectively police the chemical shenanigans of the sports world.*[8]

As Knapp pointed out in the same column: "Savvy athletes don't fear drug testing. They regard it as a small, irritating obstacle."[9]

The end result of drug testing is often cynicism toward those who are suspected, but not caught. If the tests cannot accurately catch all who violate the rules, the fairness of the procedure is open to question. Without testing, however, rules limiting performance-enhancing drugs would be irrelevant.

Matter of Privacy

The National Hockey League (NHL) adopted
a performance-enhancing drug-testing program
in 2005. Without much evidence of a significant
drug problem, the league stopped at urine tests and
did not request the blood samples needed to detect
certain illegal substances, such as Human Growth
Hormone (HGH). "We're a ways away from asking
players for a blood sample," stated Bill Daly, the
NHL deputy commissioner.[10]

With or without evidence of potential problems,
there are debates over how to weigh the invasion
of privacy of individual athletes against the goal of
creating a level playing field for all involved.

As drug testing extends down to the high school
level in some parts of the United States, the debate
continues. In 2002, the Supreme Court ruled by
a 5–4 vote that school officials' responsibility for
health and safety can outweigh students' privacy
concerns. Schools now can require random drug
tests for students who participate in extracurricular
activities.

Some states allowed the tests, but the Washington
Supreme Court ruled in 2008 that random drug
testing of student athletes through urine samples

is not allowed under that state's constitution. In handing down the ruling, the court determined:

> *A student athlete has a genuine and fundamental privacy interest in controlling his or her own bodily functions. . . . [E]ven if done in an enclosed stall, this is a significant intrusion on a student's fundamental right of privacy.*[11]

Gene Gieselmann, part of the Taylor Hooton Foundation, supports a bill that would allow for screening of high school athletes for steroid use.

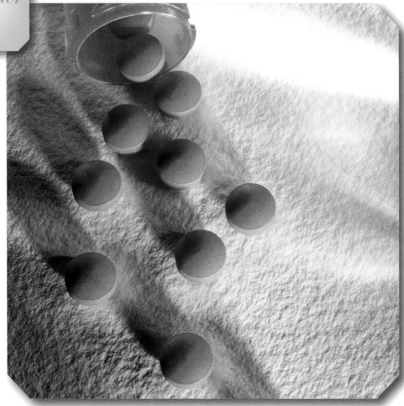

The U.S. government has spent much time and energy on the investigation of illegal steroid use.

IN THE FUTURE

Congress, through hearings in 2005 and 2008, has made clear its intentions of monitoring the processes through which major professional sports leagues in the United States attempt to control the use of performance-enhancing drugs. What remains to be determined is whether government involvement and increased attention to the subject can produce more effective results than professional leagues and international sports governing bodies. These organizations have struggled to keep up with those who try to circumvent established rules.

Bobby Rush, a Democrat from Illinois, is the chairman of the House Energy and Commerce Subcommittee on Commerce, Trade, and Consumer Protection. Rush said the subcommittee is prepared to propose legislation to attempt to stop the use of performance-enhancing drugs at all levels. He remarked:

> *If Congress can play a role in shaping public policy to eradicate all sports at every level of these substances, then the subcommittee is prepared to act. I resent all the elitists and cultural critics who dismiss this as an issue of populist spectacle. I believe we can move forward in a measured, deliberative and partisan manner with the legislation that seriously tackles drugs in sports.*[1]

Through its hearings with officials from the professional football, baseball, basketball, and hockey leagues, as well as their players' unions,

Congress continued to push for improved drug testing. The leagues were warned that if their programs were not deemed sufficient, government involvement could be next in what can be viewed as a public health issue as well as a matter of fair competition.

Frustrated by Battle

Charles Yesalis is a professor at Penn State University. He has written about performance-enhancing drugs in sports for more than two decades. He said a lot of experts believe a large percentage of record holders in sports have done so with the benefit of drugs.

The various ways to improve performance through drugs, both clearly illegal and in ways open to debate on legality, have left Yesalis wondering if it is worth bothering to try to control the situation:

"There is no commitment to stopping the drug problem. People know the sport is dirty. The sport is so driven by records."[2]
—Carl Lewis, U.S. track-and-field star and Olympic champion

Just because of my own value system, I have never seriously entertained legalizing drugs. But the stench of the hypocrisy is starting to outweigh my hesitation to just throw up my hands and say, "Let everybody do whatever they want."[3]

STARTING EARLY

While attempts are being made to try to control and catch users in professional and elite amateur sports, increased emphasis is being placed on teen athletes. Educational programs, and even high school drug testing in some states, are aimed at stopping teens from using performance-enhancing drugs or convincing them not to start.

Examples of this approach are the expansion of the ATLAS and ATHENA programs through increased financing from the National Football League (NFL) and efforts by the Taylor Hooton Foundation. Dale Murphy is a two-time National League Most Valuable Player during his baseball career with the Atlanta Braves. He has created the I WON'T CHEAT! Foundation to help eliminate drugs from sports.

Murphy said it is possible to create a culture among emerging professional athletes where cheating is not worth the risk of punishment. As an example, he says that baseball's clear intolerance of

More Tests for High School Students

When Illinois announced plans to add drug testing for high school athletes in the 2008–2009 school year, it became the fourth state to have testing by its high school sports association.

New Jersey was the first, in 2006. Florida and Texas followed.

gambling on the sport has convinced most players to avoid the risk.

> *We need better testing, harsher punishments and people will decide not to get involved with performance-enhancing drugs. Gambling in baseball is a perfect example. The culture of professional baseball players is the one thing they know, and the one thing they learn from the minute they sign a professional contract, is that you gamble on the game in any way, shape or form, your career will be over.*[4]

While fear of punishment is a potential deterrent, the fear is only realistic if athletes believe they can be caught. Estimates of players actually using performance-enhancing drugs run far ahead of

---

Changing Attitudes

Dick Pound, who heads the World Anti-Doping Agency (WADA), said that through education attitudes can be changed to make more athletes believe that using performance-enhancing drugs is an unnecessary risk.

. . . you just have to go through a longer educational process. When I first started to drive they didn't have mandatory seatbelt legislation. They brought it in and all the manly characters filled with testosterone said, "I don't need this seatbelt, I can just go 100 miles into a wall and pull myself off the steering [wheel]." And there were fines and losing points if you got caught without it, but it wasn't the fines and it wasn't the lost points that eventually got people to buckle up. It was the fact that it finally dawned on you that it's really stupid to be out there without a seatbelt on. And that's the kind of re-engineering or re-education that I think we need for sport, and it has to be directed at athletes, coaches, doctors and the public at large.[5]

the number of players caught in drug tests. As sports authorities try to find more efficient ways to test for Human Growth Hormone (HGH), other laboratories will be busy devising ways to beat that test or creating a new product altogether.

Jose Canseco said the use of steroids and other drugs should just be accepted with an emphasis on how athletes can use them as safely as possible.

In his book, *Juiced: Wild Times, Rampant 'Roids, Smash Hits, and How Baseball Got Big*, Canseco wrote:

> *We're talking about the future here. I have no doubt whatsoever that intelligent, informed use of steroids, combined with human growth hormone, will one day be so accepted that everybody will be doing it. Steroid use will be more common than Botox is now. Every baseball player and pro athlete will be using at least low levels of steroids.*[6]

Canseco's Disclaimer

Jose Canseco makes clear in his book, *Juiced,* that he thinks steroids can be effective if used properly, but cautions athletes not to start while still growing. The foreword also includes a liability disclaimer to keep Canseco and the publisher, HarperCollins, from being held responsible for adverse effects anyone might experience from taking Canseco's advice.

The disclaimer, in part, reads: "This book does not intend to condone or encourage the use of any particular drugs, medicine, or illegal substances. It is based on the personal experiences, research, and observations of the author, who is not a qualified medical professional. This book is intended to be informational and by no means should be considered to offer medical advice of any kind. It is recommended that people seek the advice of a physician before embarking on any medical treatment or exercise or training regimen."[7]

Boston Red Sox pitcher Curt Schilling is among those who believe Canseco's view of the situation sends a dangerous message. Schilling stated:

> *A book which devotes hundreds of pages to glorifying steroid usage, in which he contends steroid usage is justified and will be the norm in this country in several years, is a disgrace, was written irresponsibly and sends the opposite message that needs to be sent to kids.* [8]

Schilling also said the increased attention on steroid use could be used to control the issue: "I think the fear of public embarrassment and humiliation upon being caught is going to be greater than any player ever imagined." [9]

Don Hooton urged lawmakers to keep pursuing the issue. "Let me implore you to take steps to clean up this mess," Hooton said during a congressional hearing. "Please help us to see that our children's lives were not lost in vain." [10]

Even though the long-term effects of steroid use are unclear, professional sports organizations will continue to test their athletes.

TIMELINE

1960	1975	1976
Sports Illustrated publishes "Our Drug-Happy Athletes," exposing the use of amphetamines and other drugs by athletes.	The International Olympic Committee places anabolic steroids on its banned substances list.	The Olympics include drug testing for the first time. East Germany set eight world records during the games in Montreal, Canada.

1992	1998	1998
Lyle Alzado, who blamed his brain cancer on the use of steroids and human growth hormone, dies on May 14.	The Tour de France loses about half its competitors when performance-enhancing drugs are found.	Steve Wilstein reports that Mark McGwire has androstenedione in his locker.

1988

Canada's Ben Johnson sets a sprinting world record on September 24 but is disqualified later for testing positive for an anabolic steroid.

1990

Congress passes the Anabolic Steroids Control Act on November 29.

1991

Former East German coaches confirm they administered anabolic steroids to their swimmers in the 1970s.

1999

The World Anti-Doping Agency is formed on February 4 to oversee drug testing in sports.

2003

Taylor Hooton, a high school pitcher from Texas, commits suicide on July 15. His father blames depression brought on by steroid use.

2003

Federal investigators raid the Bay Area Laboratory Co-Operative on September 3.

TIMELINE

2004

On March 11, the U.S. Food and Drug Administration orders 23 companies to stop distributing products containing androstenedione.

2004

Ken Caminiti, a former baseball MVP who confessed to steroid use during his award-winning season, dies of a heart attack on October 10.

2005

Jose Canseco's book tells of his extensive steroid use.

2007

Professional wrestler Chris Benoit, his wife, and son are found dead on June 25. Police rule Benoit killed his family and committed suicide.

2007

Barry Bonds of the San Francisco Giants hits his 756th home run on August 7 to become Major League Baseball's career leader.

2007

On December 12, U.S. Olympic sprinter and jumper Marion Jones is stripped of the medals she won. She had admitted to steroid use.

2005

Congress conducts a hearing on March 17 and calls Jose Canseco and Mark McGwire to testify.

2006

In March, Mark Fainaru-Wada and Lance Williams release the book *Game of Shadows,* detailing the BALCO scandal.

2006

On July 27, U.S. cyclist Floyd Landis tests positive for high levels of testosterone. He is later disqualified as the Tour de France winner.

2007

The Mitchell Report is released on December 13, linking Major League Baseball players to performance-enhancing drugs.

2008

Roger Clemens and his trainer, Brian McNamee, testify February 13 in a House Committee hearing on steroid use in baseball.

2008

U.S. track-and-field star Marion Jones begins serving a six-month sentence on March 7 for lying to BALCO investigators.

Essential Facts

At Issue

Opposed

❖ The use of performance-enhancing drugs is cheating and gives an unfair advantage. It also encourages those who do not use these substances to try them in order to keep up with others who are using.

❖ Performance-enhancing drugs have significant health risks, especially on bodies that are still growing and developing.

❖ Many of these drugs are illegal in the United States without a prescription.

❖ The use of performance-enhancing drugs by professional athletes becomes an example that might be followed by younger athletes.

In Favor

❖ Performance-enhancing drugs are part of the competition involved in sports, and should be allowed as the next step in building strength, power, and endurance.

❖ An athlete has a right to privacy and should be allowed to use whatever substances he or she wishes in order to remain competitive.

❖ Unauthorized drug abuse in sports is already occurring in mass numbers. Legalized use of performance-enhancing drugs would regulate drug use and give the opportunity for all athletes to have the same resources for competition.

❖ Research on long-term effects is unclear. The dangers can be exaggerated or could be limited through proper use.

CRITICAL DATES

September 24, 1988
Canada's Ben Johnson set a world record in the 100-meter dash in 9.79 seconds at the Olympics in Seoul, South Korea, only to be disqualified two days later for testing positive for an anabolic steroid.

September 3, 2003
Federal investigators raided the Bay Area Laboratory Co-Operative (BALCO) in Burlingame, California. Baseball all-stars and track-and-field record holders were connected to the use of an undetectable steroid developed by BALCO founder Victor Conte. Baseball home run champion Barry Bonds and Olympic track champion Marion Jones were among those implicated.

December 13, 2007
The Mitchell Report, an investigation authorized by Major League Baseball, linked dozens of players, including seven-time Cy Young Award winner Roger Clemens, to performance-enhancing drugs.

February 13, 2008
Roger Clemens and his trainer, Brian McNamee, were among those called to testify in a hearing conducted by the House Committee on Oversight and Government Reform.

QUOTES

"The use of performance-enhancing drugs is not accidental; it is planned and deliberate with the sole objective of getting an unfair advantage."—*World Anti-Doping Agency chairman Dick Pound*

"This record is not tainted at all. At all. Period."—*San Francisco Giants outfielder Barry Bonds after setting the Major League Baseball career home run record August 7, 2007*

ADDITIONAL RESOURCES

SELECT BIBLIOGRAPHY

Bouton, Jim. *Ball Four*. New York: Wiley, 1990.

Canseco, Jose. *Juiced: Wild Times, Rampant 'Roids, Smash Hits, and How Baseball Got Big*. New York: HarperCollins Publishers, 2005.

Carroll, Will. *The Juice: The Real Story of Baseball's Drug Problems*. Chicago: Ivan R. Dee, 2007.

Fainaru-Wada, Mark, and Lance Williams. *Game of Shadows*. New York: Gotham Books, 2006.

FURTHER READING

Carroll, Will. *The Juice: The Real Story of Baseball's Drug Problems*. Chicago: Ivan R. Dee, 2007.

Egendorf, Laura K. *Performance-Enhancing Drugs*. San Diego: Referencepoint Press, 2007.

Rutstein, Jeff. *The Steroid Deceit: A Body Worth Dying For?* Boston: Custom Fitness Publishing, 2006.

Web Links

To learn more about performance-enhancing drugs, visit ABDO Publishing Company on the World Wide Web at **www.abdopublishing.com**. Web sites about performance-enhancing drugs are featured on our Book Links page. These links are routinely monitored and updated to provide the most current information available.

For More Information

For more information on this subject, contact or visit the following organizations.

The Taylor Hooton Foundation

6009 West Parker Road, Suite 149 Box 138, Plano, TX 75093
972-403-7300
www.taylorhooton.org
The Taylor Hooton Foundation sets out to educate about the dangers of steroids and other performance-enhancing drugs, with the goal of eliminating them from use. Its members specifically target high school and junior high school athletes.

U.S. Anti-Doping Agency (USADA)

1330 Quail Lake Loop, Suite 260, Colorado Springs, CO 80906-4651
866-601-2632
www.usantidoping.org
The USADA seeks to preserve the integrity of sports, competition, and athletes. The main areas of this agency's focus are research, education, testing, and results management.

GLOSSARY

amphetamines
Substances taken to boost energy.

anabolic steroids
Drugs that increase muscle mass and strength.

androstenedione (andro)
A hormone produced by the adrenal glands that is converted to testosterone and estradiol.

caffeine
A stimulant found in coffee beans, tea leaves, and other plants.

The Clear
One of the steroids designed by the Bay Area Laboratory Co-operative (BALCO).

The Cream
One of the steroids designed by the Bay Area Laboratory Co-operative (BALCO).

creatine
A compound produced by the body to help supply energy into muscles. Creatine can be ingested in nutritional supplements or protein-rich foods.

designer drugs
Drugs that are created to avoid detection in drug tests.

ephedrine
A stimulant previously found in cold and allergy medicines or weight-loss supplements.

erythropoietin (EPO)
A hormone that stimulates the production of red blood cells that increase aerobic capacity.

ethics
A set of moral principles.

human growth hormone (HGH)
> A hormone that stimulates muscle growth and helps reduce body fat.

insomnia
> An inability to fall or stay asleep.

insulin
> A hormone used to treat diabetes, but also used by some athletes in conjunction with steroids.

masking agent
> A drug or other substance taken in an attempt to hide the presence of other drugs in testing.

steroid precursor
> Substances that the body converts into anabolic steroids.

stimulants
> Drugs that can increase alertness and aggressiveness while suppressing appetite and reducing fatigue.

testosterone
> The natural hormone that builds muscle mass.

tetrahydrogestrinone (THG)
> A designer steroid that is difficult to detect in testing.

Source Notes

Chapter 1. Tainted History
1. Associated Press. "Bonds moves into eternity, assumes MLB home run record." 8 Aug. 2007. *ESPN.com*. 9 May 2008 <http://sports.espn.go.com/mlb/news/story?id=2965584>.
2. Ibid.
3. Ibid.
4. Ibid.
5. "Bonds exposed." 7 Mar. 2006. *SI.com*. 9 May 2008 <http://sportsillustrated.cnn.com/2006/baseball/mlb/03/06/news.excerpt/index.html>.

Chapter 2. The Temptation
1. "Taking performance-enhancing drugs: Are you risking your health?" *MayoClinic.com*. 27 Mar. 2008 <http://www.mayoclinic.com/health/performance-enhancing-drugs/HQ01105>.
2. Ibid.
3. "The enforcer." 19 Jan. 2003. *CBC Sports*. 10 May 2008 <http://www.cbc.ca/sports/indepth/drugs/stories/qa_dickpound.html>.
4. Jeffrey Katz. "Should We Accept Steroid Use in Sports?" 23 Jan. 2008. *npr.com*. 10 May 2008 <http://www.npr.org/templates/story/story.php?storyId=18299098>.
5. Ibid.
6. Ibid.
7. Ibid.
8. Ibid.

Chapter 3. Steroids, Hormones, and Stimulants
1. Maggie Fox and Dan Trotta. "Why use steroids? They work." 13 Dec. 2007. *Reuters.com*. 10 May 2008 <http://www.reuters.com/article/topNews/idUSN1320020520071213>.
2. "Anabolic Steroids." *ESPN.com*. 18 Apr. 2008 <http://espn.go.com/special/s/drugsandsports/steroids.html>.
3. Ibid.
4. "Feds Crack Down on Andro Sales." 11 Mar. 2004. *Associated Press/CBS News*. 10 May 2008 <http://www.cbsnews.com/stories/2004/03/11/health/main605300.shtml>.

Chapter 4. Baseball's Issues Become Public
1. Carlos Frias. "Baseball and amphetamines." 2 Apr. 2006. *Palm Beach Post*. 10 May 2008 <http://www.palmbeachpost.com/sports/content/sports/epaper/2006/04/02/PBP_AMPHET_0402.html>.
2. Ibid.
3. "10 Burning Questions for Jim Bouton." *ESPN.com*. 18 Apr. 2008 <http://espn.go.com/page2/s/questions/bouton.html>.
4. "Questions and Answers: Androstenedione." 11 Mar. 2004. *Food and Drug*

Administration Online. 10 May 2008 <http://www.cfsan.fda.gov/~dms/androqa. html>.

5. Rebecca Shore. "A timeline of performance-enhancing drugs in sports." 11 Mar. 2008. *SI.com.* 9 May 2008 <http://sportsillustrated.cnn.com/2008/ magazine/03/11/steroid.timeline/index.html>.

6. Jorge Arangure Jr. "Palmeiro Suspended for Steroid Violation." 2 Aug. 2005. *Washington Post.* 9 May 2008 <http://www.washingtonpost.com/wp-dyn/ content/article/2005/08/01/AR2005080100739.html>.

7. "Clemens says he got B-12 shots; ex-trainer claims steroids." 13 Feb. 2008. *CNN.com.* 9 May 2008 <http://www.cnn.com/2008/POLITICS/02/13/ steroids.baseball/index.html>.

Chapter 5. Individual Sports

1. Belton, David. "The pariah of the sporting world." 22 July 2001. BBC News. 9 May 2008 <http://news.bbc.co.uk/1/hi/programmes/from_our_own_ correspondent/1449381.stm>

2. "Ben Johnson Confesses." 17 June 1989. *New York Times.* 9 May 2008 <http://query.nytimes.com/gst/fullpage.html?res=950DE6D61130F934A257 55C0A96F948260>.

3. Stan Grossfeld. "Johnson has been slow to admit wrongdoing." 28 Apr. 2005. *Boston Globe.* 9 May 2008 <http://www.boston.com/sports/ articles/2005/04/28/johnson_has_been_slow_to_admit_wrongdoing/>.

4. Ibid.

5. Ibid.

6. Michael Janofsky. "Coaches Concede That Steroids Fueled East Germany's Success in Swimming." 3 Dec. 1991. *New York Times.* 11 May 2008 <http:// query.nytimes.com/gst/fullpage.html?res=9D0CE1DA1731F930A35751C1 A967958260>.

7. Dave Anderson. "A Swimmer Splashes Suspicion." 23 July 1996. *New York Times.* 11 May 2008 <http://query.nytimes.com/gst/fullpage.html?res=9B06E1 D91639F930A15754C0A960958260&sec=&spon=&pagewanted=1>.

8. Associated Press. "Landis' backup doping test also positive." 5 Aug. 2006. *NBCSports.com.* 10 May 2008 <http://nbcsports.msnbc.com/id/14059185/>.

9. Janice Lloyd. "Jones' relay mates stripped of 2000 Olympic medals." 10 Apr. 2008. *USA Today.* 10 May 2008 <http://www.usatoday.com/sports/ olympics/2008-04-10-jones-mates-medals_N.htm>.

10. Associated Press. "Olympic Gold Medalist Marion Jones Pleads Guilty in Steroids Case." 5 Oct. 2007. *FOXNEWS.com.* 10 May 2008 <http://www. foxnews.com/story/0,2933,299717,00.html>.

Source Notes Continued

Chapter 6. Power Source

1. Dave Anderson. "The Undiscussed Issue: Steroid Test Loopholes." 28 Apr. 2005. *New York Times.* 10 May 2008 <http://www.nytimes.com/2005/04/28/sports/football/28anderson.html>.

2. Ibid.

3. Ibid.

4. Wallace Matthews. "NFL is getting a pass on steroid use." 20 Feb. 2008. *Newsday.* 10 May 2008 <http://www.newsday.com/sports/ny-spwally205584482feb20,0,3485877.column>.

5. Ibid.

6. Mike Puma. "Not the size of the dog in the fight." *ESPN.com.* 20 Apr. 2008 <http://espn.go.com/classic/biography/s/Alzado_Lyle.html>.

7. Ibid.

8. Ibid.

9. Jeff Barker. "Steroid use in NFL may be wider than thought." 26 Apr. 2005. *Baltimore Sun.* 10 May 2008 <http://www.baltimoresun.com/sports/football/bal-te.sp.nflsteroids26apr26,1,6973612.story?coll=bal-sports-football>.

10. Ibid.

Chapter 7. Youthful Concerns

1. "Don Hooton: Son Committed Suicide After Using Steroids." 15 July 2003. *United States Senate Online.* 11 May 2008 <http://drugcaucus.senate.gov/steroids04Hooten.html>.

2. Ibid.

3. Ibid.

4. Gailon Totheroh. "Juiced: The Frightening Rise of Teen Steroid Use." *CBN.com.* 21 Apr. 2008 <http://www.cbn.com/cbnnews/news/050420a.aspx>.

5. "Don Hooton: Son Committed Suicide After Using Steroids." 15 July 2003. *United States Senate Online.* 11 May 2008 <http://drugcaucus.senate.gov/steroids04Hooten.html>.

6. Dr. Linn Goldberg in speech at NFL Youth Summit, North Canton, Ohio. 26 July 2007.

7. Gailon Totheroh. "Juiced: The Frightening Rise of Teen Steroid Use." *CBN.com.* 21 Apr. 2008 <http://www.cbn.com/cbnnews/news/050420a.aspx>.

8. "Don Hooton: Son Committed Suicide After Using Steroids." 15 July 2003. *United States Senate Online.* 11 May 2008 <http://drugcaucus.senate.gov/steroids04Hooten.html>.

Chapter 8. Drug Testing

1. Mark Maske. "NFL, Union Beef Up Drug Program." 25 Jan. 2007. *Washington Post.* 11 May 2008 <http://www.washingtonpost.com/wp-dyn/content/article/2007/01/24/AR2007012401824.html>.

2. Ibid.

3. Associated Press. "MLB, players union agree to more frequent drug testing." 11 Apr. 2008. *ESPN.com*. 11 May 2008 <http://sports.espn.go.com/mlb/news/story?id=3341940>.

4. Ibid.

5. Ibid.

6. Lincoln Allison. "Faster, stronger, higher." 9 Aug. 2004. *The Guardian*. 11 May 2008 <http://sport.guardian.co.uk/olympics2004/story/0,,1279126,00.html>.

7. Gwen Knapp. "Tour de France has learned drug testing's not the answer." 2 July 2006. *San Francisco Chronicle*. 11 May 2008 <http://www.sfgate.com/cgi-bin/article.cgi?f=/c/a/2006/07/02/SPGLPJO6FJ1.DTL>.

8. Ibid.

9. Ibid.

10. Scott Burnside. "Debate over NHL's drug-testing policy rages on." 6 Aug. 2007. *ESPN.com*. 11 May 2008 <http://sports.espn.go.com/nhl/columns/story?columnist=burnside_scott&id=2963703>.

11. Maureen O'Hagan. "WA high court says random school drug testing unconstitutional." 13 Mar. 2008. *Seattle Times*. 11 May 2008 <http://seattletimes.nwsource.com/html/localnews/2004279865_webdrugtests13m.html>.

Chapter 9. In the Future

1. "At drugs hearing, committee vows different atmosphere." 27 Feb. 2008. *USA Today*. 11 May 2008 <http://www.usatoday.com/sports/2008-02-27-drugs-hearing_N.htm>.

2. "10 Drug Scandals." 19 Jan. 2003. *CBC Sports*. 11 May 2008 <http://www.cbc.ca/sports/indepth/drugs/stories/top10.html>.

3. Matthew Herper. "Performance Drugs Outrun The Olympics." 15 Feb. 2002. *Forbes.com*. 11 May 2008 <http://www.forbes.com/2002/02/15/0215ped.html>.

4. Jeffrey Katz. "Should We Accept Steroid Use in Sports?" *npr.com*. 27 Mar. 2008 <http://www.npr.org/templates/story/story.php?storyId=18299098>.

5. "The enforcer." 19 Jan. 2003. *CBC Sports*. 10 May 2008 <http://www.cbc.ca/sports/indepth/drugs/stories/qa_dickpound.html>.

6. Jose Canseco. *Juiced: Wild Times, Rampant 'Roids, Smash Hits, and How Baseball Got Big*. New York: HarperCollins Publishers, 2005. 2.

7. Ibid. N. pag.

8. Ted Barrett. "McGwire mum on steroids in hearing." *CNN.com*. 23 Apr. 2008 <http://www.cnn.com/2005/ALLPOLITICS/03/17/steroids.baseball/index.html>.

9. Ibid.

10. Ibid.

INDEX

ABOUT THE AUTHOR

Tom Robinson has written about sports, ranging from the professional to youth levels, for more than two decades. His report on the use of expense money within the Pennsylvania Interscholastic Athletic Association (PIAA) was named as one of the top ten news stories in the 50,000–175,000 circulation category in 1998 by the Associated Press Sports Editors. He also received media awards from Districts 2 and 12 of the PIAA. Robinson has spent time as a coach and organizer of youth and high school sports. He lives in Pennsylvania with his family.

PHOTO CREDITS